DIVORCE

DIVORCE

BY ANN S. WHITE

FRANKLIN WATTS
NEW YORK | LONDON | 1979
A FIRST BOOK

Library of Congress Cataloging in Publication Data

White, Ann S.
Divorce.

(A First book)
Includes index.
SUMMARY: Discusses the causes and procedures of divorce, the changes it brings to family life, and its effects on children.
1. Divorce — United States — Juvenile literature. 2. Children of divorced parents — United States — Juvenile literature. [1. Divorce] I. Title.
HQ834.W57 301.42'84'0973 78-10464
ISBN 0-531-02254-4

Printed in the United States of America
5 4 3

CONTENTS

To John, Diana, and Dick.
With love and hope for the future.

DIVORCE

AMY, TOM, MICHELLE, AND PETER

Amy Clark lives in a small town in Pennsylvania. She is ten, loves to play the piano, sing, and take long walks with her dog around the lake which is down the road from her house. Once a month she and her brother get on a bus and go to New York for the weekend.

Tom Simon lives in New York City. From Monday through Friday, he lives in a big apartment building near the Hudson River. His eighth-grade class is going on a trip to the Museum of Natural History this Saturday. But Tom won't go with them. Every weekend he goes to New Jersey.

Michelle and Peter Davis are eleven-year-old twins who live in California near the desert. Everyone says Michelle looks like her mother and Peter like his father. Peter's not sure, though. It's been a long time since Peter's seen his father.

What do Amy, Tom, Michelle, and Peter have in common, aside from the fact that they are children? They all have parents who have been divorced.

Perhaps your parents are divorced. Or maybe you have some friends or cousins whose parents are divorced. It's very possible because over one-third of all marriages in the United States end in divorce these days. Half of those divorces are in families with children. In fact, half of all black children and one-fourth of all white children have parents who are divorced.

Like Amy, Tom, Michelle, and Peter, these children's lives are changed by their parents' divorces. Sometimes the changes are for the better, sometimes for the worse. But always changed.

AMY

When Amy's parents divorced, she moved with her mother and brother from a house with a big yard to an apartment. She saw her father, who lived nearby, almost every Sunday. Two years later, her mother married a man who had never been married and they moved to a house in Pennsylvania. Her name is different now from her mother's and stepfather's. She thinks her stepfather is okay, but complains that he loves her mother more than he loves her and her brother. She wishes she saw more of her father. She isn't sure why her parents got divorced. She was only five then and nobody told her.

TOM

Tom lives with his father. Because his father doesn't get home from work until 7 p.m., a housekeeper is there when Tom gets home from school. He has two older sisters who live with their mother in New Jersey. But things weren't always this way. When his parents were divorced, Tom lived with his mother too. But he was really unhappy being a thirteen-year-old boy in a house filled with women. They seemed to have so many things in common and he felt very left out. Neither one of his parents has remarried and they still fight a lot whenever they talk. They fought a lot about Tom, but finally he was able to go live with his father. Tom's not sure how his father managed it. All he knows is that his parents went back to court to work it out. Most of the time

Tom thinks it's great living with his father. The only thing that bothers him is that he knows it makes his mother feel bad.

MICHELLE AND PETER

Michelle and Peter haven't seen their father since they were five years old. They heard that he got married again and moved to Arizona. They live with their mother, stepfather, and little brother. Sometimes on weekends their stepfather's other children come to visit. It can get pretty confusing. Michelle and Peter aren't sure why they don't see or hear from their father. Or why their stepfather is less strict with his real kids than with them. Sometimes being part of a big family is fun for them, but there are times when they wonder why their mother ever wanted to get married again.

Like Amy, Tom, Michelle, and Peter, most children have lots of unanswered questions about divorce.

Why does it happen? How do people get divorced? What will happen to the children? Before we can really tackle those questions, let's take a look at marriage. After all, divorce wouldn't exist if there weren't any marriages.

WHAT GOES WRONG?

Marriage used to be something people did in order to survive. They didn't have formal ceremonies, but they lived together because it made sense to stay with someone they trusted. If they didn't get along very well, the only thing that kept them from parting was fear of the hostile world outside their cave.

Today marriage is a formal pledge two people make to love one another for the rest of their lives. It is a contract that evolved from tribal customs. Then governments and religions developed and refined the terms of the contract even more to protect the couple's property and children.

People no longer decide to live together for protection from the outside world. They live together because they meet someone they like being with. That person makes them happy, and they think their lives would not be as full without the other person. They believe that they will always feel a special thrill when they are together. They are full of hope and promise for a lifetime of happiness.

Almost everyone who gets married feels this way. So what goes wrong? Why do so many of them change their minds after a few years?

Like life and death, much of why and how a divorce happens is a mystery even to those who are involved in it. Adults as well as children often have a hard time understanding exactly what went wrong in a marriage. That's why no one ever told Amy why her parents got a divorce.

When it happened, both parents were too confused about the reasons to explain things to her. Her mother could have told her that her father was leaving because he loved someone else. But she knew it was more complicated than that. So she said nothing and cried a lot. Her father said he was leaving because he didn't love her mother anymore. But he couldn't say why that happened. It was all very mysterious and Amy wondered if maybe it wasn't her fault that they split up. Of course it wasn't, but she couldn't think of any other reason.

Amy might have felt better if she knew that there are a lot of very complicated reasons why people get divorced. Here are a few of them:

Disappointment — A lot of people get divorced because their marriage is no longer romantic. A bride and groom imagine that the one they love is the answer to their dreams — a really wonderful person. Thinking this makes them feel more important too. After all, if such a wonderful person loves you, then you must be terrific too. This kind of love hides the ways in which the bride and groom differ. It is called romantic love, and it has a hard time surviving the everyday difficulties of a marriage. It's not that there is anything really wrong with romantic love. All healthy, happy marriages contain a lot of romance mixed with reality. The problem lies in the great expectations of romantic love. People often say of newly married people, "They seem like the perfect couple." A lot of people expect to be part of the perfect couple. When they realize they are not, they can't bear to substitute reality for the dream and they go in search of another romantic love.

Incompatibility — Many people cannot get along because of different temperaments and different attitudes toward sex, money, or religion. The couple who lovingly said "I do" couldn't imagine on their wedding day that there might come a time when they would disagree on what to eat, when to make love, whether or not to go to church, where to go on vacation, or how much to spend on whatever they would want to buy. Even people of similar backgrounds have very different points of view on many of the day-to-day aspects of married life.

Because of these differences, they fight, sometimes just with words, occasionally with fists. Their love turns to bitterness, anger, and revenge. Some of them leave home, either alone or on the arm of someone new.

Changing needs — Some people marry for very unhealthy reasons. They are lonely and think they can count on someone else to cure that loneliness. Some people need to suffer, so they marry people who hurt them through alcoholism, drug addiction, beatings, humiliation, etc. Others have to help someone they feel is less fortunate and they marry people they think need them desperately. A lot of marriages based on unhealthy needs fall apart if one of the partners changes his or her needs. Picture, for instance, what would happen when a woman marries a man primarily because he represents security for her. She counts on him to take care of her because she feels helpless to take care of herself. And perhaps her husband needs to feel that he is counted on to provide security. Everything may be fine until the day he loses his job or has a heart attack and needs her to take care of him. Unless both can adapt to the new roles life demands of them, the marriage may very well end.

The changing role of women is having a similar effect on many marriages. Men who were brought up to believe that a woman's place is in the home often are confronted with their wives' desire to go back to work or continue their careers. Unable to adjust to this change in their expectation of a wife, they get divorced.

Undoing a bad decision — Some people get divorced because they never really wanted to marry their husband or wife in the first place. They did it because they thought they had to. Teenagers who get married only because they are about to have a baby are a good example. Teenage marriages account for the largest number of divorces, many of them for this reason. Some homosexuals, people who prefer their own sex, get married because they think that's what society expects them to do.

Attitudes have changed a lot in the last few years. Now there is less pressure on people to get married.

ISN'T THERE ANYTHING THEY CAN DO TO WORK OUT THEIR PROBLEMS?

Yes. Before rushing out to hire a divorce lawyer, there are two important things a couple can do when their marriage is in trouble.

COUNSELING

The first thing they can do is to get professional counseling. There are several different kinds of counselors. Some of them will meet with the whole family. Others will see a husband and wife together. Some will see only one of the two partners. This list should give you an idea of who they are and what they do:

Psychiatrists — Some psychiatrists are trained in marital counseling, but most are not. A psychiatrist has a medical degree. Besides being a doctor, he or she has had at least three years of training in taking care of people who are mentally ill, probably in a mental institution.

Psychoanalysts — These are psychiatrists who take additional courses in psychoanalysis. Only a small percentage of psychiatrists offer joint counseling for husband and wife. They usually will see only one of them.

Clinical Psychologists — These counselors have a Ph.D. (Doctor of Philosophy) degree in clinical psychology. Most of them have some training in counseling and a few specialize in family therapy. They will treat patients alone, as a couple, or sometimes in groups.

Social Workers — These counselors are qualified to do counseling if they have specialized in psychiatric social work and have an M.S.W. (Master of Social Work) degree.

While they are in graduate school, they work in an agency or hospital that offers counseling.

Church or Pastoral Counselors — This group includes ministers, priests, and rabbis who have had advanced training in psychology or counseling. For a long time, pastoral counselors had more experience than actual formal training. Lately, many more members of the clergy are studying for a Master's degree in psychology before they do counseling.

The most effective type of counseling is different for each couple. Counseling doesn't guarantee that the marriage will be saved. It does, however, help people to understand their behavior. If their behavior is causing problems in their marriage, counseling may teach them new ways to behave.

Counselors can't work miracles. They can help when people have a strong desire to work out their differences. If a couple does split up, counseling may help them through the emotional confusion of a divorce.

Some states require counseling before a divorce can be granted. They hope that at least a few people will be helped and decide not to get a divorce. This doesn't work very often. Counseling helps most when it is voluntary.

SEPARATION

Another thing people can do is separate for a while. Separation may look like divorce because the couple isn't living together, but it is different because it is not final. It doesn't break the marriage contract.

Sometimes people need to get away from one another to remember the good things about their marriage. Daily fighting or constant financial worries can make them forget the happy times they used to have. Separation can give them a chance to look at their marriage in a different way. It can help them decide that they want to work to keep the marriage together.

Some couples combine counseling and separation. They discover new ways to treat each other that can make them happier. That doesn't mean they won't ever fight. It means that they will still appreciate each other even though they won't always agree on everything.

Some separations are formal court orders, but most are just temporary living arrangements to see if being apart is better than being together.

Separation can, however, work to keep a married couple together. For example, one couple had been very unhappy for about a year. For a while they fought. They yelled and slammed doors. Then they just stopped talking to each other except when they had to. Their children felt the tension between the parents and were very unhappy too.

The mother decided to go for counseling, but not to save the marriage. She thought it might help her take charge of her own life. She began to understand a lot of things about her marriage through counseling. But because they hadn't talked in a long time, she couldn't discuss these things with her husband.

They finally separated, and she moved to another state. With some distance between them, the parents were able to start talking again. At first, they spoke over the phone after the children had talked to their dad. Then they met in person and found they enjoyed being together again. Finally, they got around to talking about a way to rebuild their marriage. They were able to choose a whole new way of life that is much better for their marriage. They believe this would not have happened if they hadn't gotten away from each other. The separation gave them a chance to break some bad habits.

TO BLAME OR NOT TO BLAME

Amy's parents got a "No Fault" divorce. Tom's mother sued his father for mental cruelty. Michelle and Peter's mother claimed desertion. What do all these terms mean? Why can't people just say they don't get along?

Most civilizations over the centuries have encouraged marriage. Through their customs and eventually through their laws, they discouraged divorce. So besides trying to cope with their personal problems, people who want a divorce have to weave through a maze of laws.

Historically, divorce was an adversary procedure — a fight in which one of the two people had to be found guilty and then punished. In the United States, divorce is still often granted only when one person proves the other to be at fault. What he or she is being accused of is called "grounds."

Here are some typical grounds for a divorce under the "fault" system:

Adultery — This is when a married person voluntarily has sexual relations with someone other than the person to whom he or she is married. Adultery is considered grounds for divorce in every state.

Although adultery is one of the well-known grounds for divorce, it isn't used too often because people are embarrassed to go into court and publicly announce that their mate has been unfaithful. Often parents do not want their children to learn that one of them has committed adultery.

Desertion — This occurs when one partner voluntarily leaves the other without good reason and without the other's consent. Temporary absence because of business or even separation for the purpose of getting a divorce is not considered desertion. Usually, there is a one- to five-year time period before desertion can be considered grounds for a divorce. About one-third of all divorces are granted on the grounds of desertion.

Cruelty — The definition of cruelty as grounds for divorce states that there must be bodily harm or a reasonable fear of bodily injury inflicted by one partner on the other. Hurt feelings don't count.

Most states actually allow people to use cruelty as grounds for an uncontested divorce even though there has been no physical brutality in their marriage. They do this because they recognize that there are very complex ways in which people inflict pain on one another. Sometimes alcoholism and drug addiction fall into the category of cruelty. In other states, these are listed as separate grounds. Homosexual behavior on the part of a partner is often considered cruelty by the courts.

About half of all divorces in the United States are granted on the grounds of cruelty.

Adultery, desertion, and cruelty are the major "fault" grounds for divorce. Some states allow divorce on the grounds of non-support, incurable insanity, or a felony conviction. Occasionally, a court may decide that both parties are guilty and no divorce would be granted.

"NO FAULT"

Lately, however, many states have recognized that the reasons marriages fail are more complex than the traditional grounds for divorce. They have changed their laws to allow what is known as a "no fault" divorce. Instead of having to prove that a spouse was guilty of wrongdoing, a couple can get a divorce on the basis of not being able to get along. Sometimes the law refers to no fault grounds as "incompatibility" or "irretrievable breakdown of the marriage relationship", or "irreconcilable differences." Three states — Colorado, Florida, and Indiana — no longer even use the term "divorce." They use the term "Dissolution of Marriage," meaning that the marriage is simply dissolved. Most states that offer no fault divorce also offer traditional fault grounds. That is because a no fault divorce must be uncontested. This means both parties must agree on the terms of the divorce: custody, financial settlements, etc. And many people who can't get along well enough to live together cannot agree on the terms of their divorce either.

There are some advantages to no fault divorce, though, that make it worth choosing. It is often faster, cheaper, and less bitter. No fault allows people to divorce with dignity, without public scandal, and with no reason to lie under oath just so the state will allow them to part when their marriage has broken down.

Sometimes people who choose a no fault divorce do so because they feel the fault lies with both of them. They accept the fact that they both made mistakes or drifted apart, and they choose to divorce in a way that has more compassion than anger.

Regardless of the grounds, most people do not divorce

in haste. Usually, several months to many years go by from the time they decide they want to get out of their marriage. Divorce isn't something that just happens. It is a process involving many events.

HOW DO PEOPLE ACTUALLY GET A DIVORCE?

The first thing they do is hire a lawyer to help them break the marriage contract. The lawyer prepares the necessary documents for a divorce. If the situation is complicated, the lawyer's help can be very expensive. A divorce may cost anywhere from a few hundred dollars to many thousands of dollars just for lawyers' fees. This depends on the amount of time it takes the lawyers to help divorcing couples settle their disagreements.

The first document a lawyer prepares is called a Complaint for Divorce. It includes a request for a divorce and the following information:

1. Names of the parties involved
2. When and how long they were married
3. Number and ages of their children, if any
4. When the partners separated
5. The value of their property
6. The needs of the parties
7. The grounds for divorce

A lawyer's job is to help a couple settle out of court. Most people, in fact over 90 per cent, eventually settle out of court. If, however, a couple cannot agree on all the terms of the divorce, the terms will be settled by a judge. Hardly ever is a jury used to settle a divorce case. A judge will study all the evidence, and may require that a couple have counseling, and eventually will decide how much property each gets, who gets custody of any children, and how often the other parent will see the children.

Some of the most difficult problems for a divorcing couple to settle are financial. The laws regarding financial settlements are part of a tradition that began in English courts in the 1600s. No divorces were granted then, only permission to live apart. In those days a woman was not allowed to own property. Everything she had belonged to her husband. When they separated, her husband had a continued responsibility to support her. This support is called **alimony.**

Most states still require a man to pay his former wife alimony (as long as she remains unmarried) because for many years in the history of the United States, women were not able to earn enough money to live on.

Now that it is possible for women to support themselves through work, the practice of paying alimony is changing somewhat. If a woman is equipped to support herself, she may not get alimony. We live in a time of transition and heated argument on this subject. There are those who say that alimony represents a kind of payment to a woman for years of household services rendered in the marriage. Others want to abolish alimony because they believe it keeps women dependent upon a former spouse. Some courts have even argued that in cases where a woman's financial position is superior to that of her former husband, he should receive support from her.

In general, alimony is based on need, a spouse's ability to pay, length of the marriage, and in some cases punishment for misconduct.

As you can see, the subject of alimony can be one of the most difficult to agree on during a divorce. Once it is settled, there are laws to ensure that the agreement is upheld. These laws are often difficult and expensive to enforce, however.

When there are children in a marriage that has ended, a couple must agree on their support. Support payments usually continue only until a child reaches an agreed-upon age such as eighteen or twenty-one, unlike alimony which might last a spouse's lifetime. Support payments often cover more than food, shelter, and clothing. They might include the cost of medical care, education, and summer camp. Usually, child support is sent to the parent with whom the child lives, not to the child. If that puzzles you, it is done that way because the parent pays the bills for all those things we mentioned. Most people pay child support more willingly than alimony.

WHO GETS THE CHILDREN?

For practical reasons, children of divorced parents usually live with one parent, the one who has "custody." Amy, Michelle, and Peter live in their mother's custody. Tom's mother originally had custody of him. Then his father went back to court and asked the judge to give him custody of Tom.

Custody is usually settled out of court. The parents talk it over and decide where the children should live. Most children under eighteen live with their mothers. That's because the tradition in this country has been for mothers to provide most of the daily care for children, while the fathers left the house to go to work. When a mother worked too, it was still her responsibility to care for the children. Modern families tend to share more of the responsibility for child care, but especially when a child is very young, the law recognizes that it is the mother who usually spends the most time with the child.

If parents cannot settle the issue of custody out of court, the court has the power to tell them where the children will live. There are two general rules the court uses to determine custody:

1. What is best for the welfare and happiness of the child
2. Which parent is considered not "at fault" by the law

The courts will consider the age, health, and sex of the child. Sometimes, when a teenager is involved, they will consider his or her preference.

What happened in Tom's family is a good example. When his parents were divorced, the court decided that Tom and his two sisters should live with their mother. Judges usually do not think it's a good idea to divide up the children between parents. At that time, Tom was nine years old and his sisters were eleven and thirteen.

By the time Tom turned twelve, he had grown to be a moody, rebellious child. He was having trouble in school and was constantly fighting with his mother and sisters. Tom hated being the only male in a house full of females. He wanted to live with his father.

His mother and father fought about it. His mother didn't want him to leave. Tom's father went to court and told the judge why he thought Tom would be better off living with him. He said that Tom's behavior showed that living in an all-female house wasn't good for him. He convinced the judge that Tom was old enough to survive without his mother's daily care, and he proved that he could provide a proper upbringing for Tom.

Now that Tom's father was going to have Tom with him, the judge also agreed that the father could send less child support money to his ex-wife.

Although courts usually give custody to parents, sometimes they give it to grandparents or to the state. The state has custody when the parents are unable to take care of the children. This doesn't happen very often.

A new type of custody arrangement is being tried by some people. Divorcing parents who live in the same neighborhood (and the same school district) arrange for their children to spend half the week in one home and half in the other. This is called shared custody.

A CHANCE TO VISIT

Even though one parent has custody, the other is permitted to visit the children regularly. You may have friends like Amy and Tom who aren't always home on weekends. Or you may know kids like Michelle and Peter who haven't seen one of their parents in a long time. You may wonder why it is that some kids don't see one parent very much. And you may wonder what it is like to visit with someone you used to live with.

Well, first of all, visiting rights, like custody, can be settled out of court. Or the court can decide on how often the children will see their absent parent. Courts are usually more than fair in giving visitation rights to the absent parent. Most court orders just say that the parent is entitled to "reasonable" visitation rights. In addition, they may spell out the days and times of the visits. What happens after that depends upon how well everyone cooperates.

Amy's parents usually cooperate fairly well. When Amy's mother remarried and moved to Pennsylvania, Amy was afraid she might not see her father very much. It took a while before she and her brother got used to once-a-month visits with their father. The way things are now, they visit him over most long weekends and school vacations. In the summer, they go on a two-week vacation with him. They use visiting time well and have a growing and close relationship with their father. In Amy's situation, the parents, her stepfather, and the two children are all working to make visitation a good experience. They all agree that children need to know their father.

Some parents use visitation rights as a way of bargaining during and after a divorce. Some mothers threaten that if they do not get a certain amount of money for support, or if they don't get to keep property they want, the father will not be able to see his children very much. Or the father may say that if he can't have custody he will refuse to support his ex-wife. They do these things because they are angry at being rejected or because they want material comforts for themselves or for their children. This kind of behavior creates enormous bitterness and hurts everyone involved, especially the children. That's the kind of thing that went on in Tom's house.

A few fathers, like Michelle and Peter's, have a hard time keeping up a relationship with their children after a divorce. Sometimes they feel awkward and don't know how to act around them. Sometimes they stop seeing their children because they are bitter toward their ex-wife and don't want to see her. Other fathers feel guilty because they think they caused the divorce. They may believe their children are better off without them. They forget that kids need both of their parents. Children like Michelle and Peter sometimes wonder what is wrong with them that could cause their mother or father to go away and forget about them. But there is nothing wrong with Michelle and Peter. The problem is that not all parents are responsible, wise, and unselfish.

Visiting someone you used to live with can feel strange at first. Sometimes nobody knows how to act. Some parents act like Santa Claus. They give their children lots of presents as a substitute for spending time with them. Or they plan every visit to be all fun and games. After all, that sure beats the real life you have at home. Or does it? It would probably be more fun if parents and children could be more relaxed with one another.

There is sometimes a lot of competition between divorced parents for their children's love. A little bit of this is probably normal, but sometimes it reaches extremes.

One parent may try to turn a child against the other parent. A mother may say: "Your father is a horrible person. But I'm sure that you will never turn out like him." Or a father may say: "Your mother never did have much of a sense of humor." It may seem fairly innocent, but it's often part of the game to make a child take sides.

It's hard for children to avoid getting caught in the middle. Wise and loving parents will do their best to avoid putting their children in that position. They will use custody and visitation in ways that will help their children mature into healthy adults.

DON'T THE CHILDREN HAVE ANY RIGHTS?

By now you're probably asking, "But what about the children? Don't they have anything to say about where they live or when they see their other parent?"

The truth is that they usually don't. Occasionally, a child in his or her mid-teens, for example, might be able to choose. And then only if his or her parents agree, and if the court agrees. Usually, the courts and psychologists believe it is unfair to ask children to choose which parent they want to live with. They think children would worry about hurting the parent they didn't choose. Look at Tom. He was miserable living with his mother, and he chose to live with his father for some very good reasons. But he still felt guilty about his mother's feelings.

The courts try to make custody arrangements they think are best for the children. Some states have adopted a Bill of Rights for Children in the case of divorce. These are guidelines to help make sure children of divorced parents have a good and loving home to grow up in. They also try to make sure children will have a chance to know and love both their parents and have the same opportunities they would have had if their parents hadn't gotten a divorce.

DIVORCE CAN BE A BEGINNING

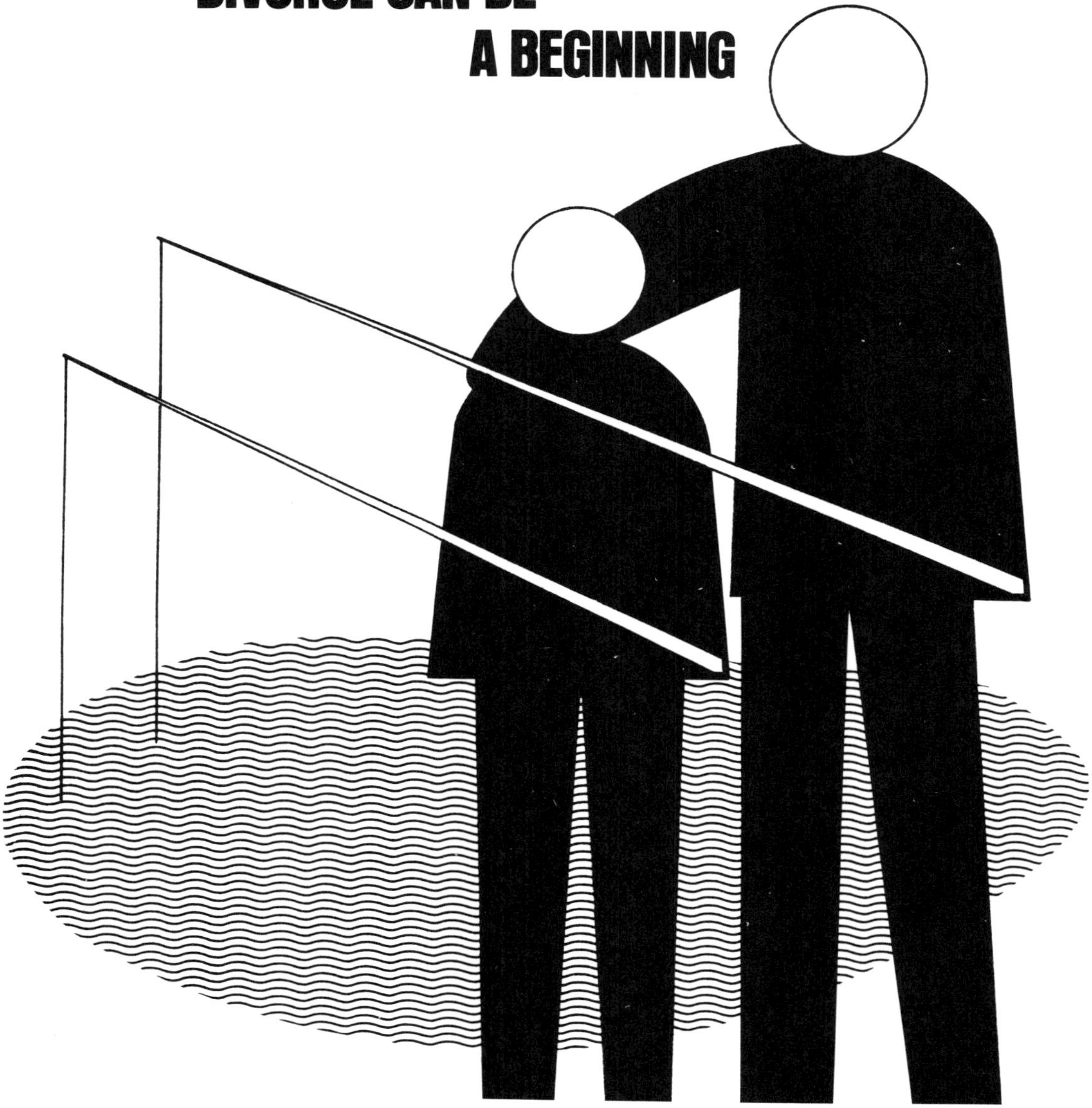

Young people find it hard to think of divorce as a way of settling problems. That's because from their point of view divorce causes so many changes.

Aside from the very basic problems of custody and visitation, there are some other kinds of changes that affect children when their parents divorce.

MOVING

When people divorce, the money which once provided one home now has to pay for two homes. That's the reason one of the first things that usually happens to children when their family splits up is that they move. Usually, they move to an apartment or house that is smaller and less expensive. This happens even though the parents may realize that emotionally it isn't a good thing to do. They just may not have any other choice.

The parent and children pack up, move out, and leave behind familiar faces and places. Sometimes moving is a great adventure. Or it can be a real disappointment. Lots of times it just depends on how you look at it.

For a lot of children whose parents have just divorced, moving is hard because it increases their feelings of loneliness. Getting involved in school and neighborhood clubs can make things easier. But most of all, time helps.

COPING WITH A WORKING PARENT

For many children, it is nothing new to live with working parents. Many mothers as well as fathers hold full-time jobs.

But for others, a divorce may mean that the mother who used to be there when they came home from school now gets home from work at 6 p.m. Children may come home to a babysitter or an empty house. The same thing is true if a child is in his father's custody, as we saw in the case of Tom Simon.

Lots of parents come home from work very tired and feeling that they need to relax for a few minutes. When there is only one parent in the home, it's extra hard to find time to do that. The children have been waiting to talk to the parent, the sitter may need a ride home, dinner must be cooked, and the house cleaned. What should be a pleasant evening together can often be full of tension and short tempers.

Single parents who work may expect their children to do chores that never had to be done before (by the kids, that is). Lots of children resent this. But most single working parents ask their children to assume some extra responsibility.

A CHANCE TO GET TO KNOW YOUR PARENTS

Even though there are a lot of changes to adjust to after a divorce, it can be the beginning of a new and better relationship with each parent. Because they live apart, a child can get to know them individually, not just as part of a team.

The important thing is to be honest with your parents and make the most of an opportunity to get to know them. If visits with an absent parent are disappointing, it might be because the parent doesn't understand that a child might prefer to spend time talking rather than going to the movies. If the child never tells the parent about the need to talk, they'll probably spend the rest of their lives sitting through movies together.

DATING

As much as parents love their children, they will probably want to have an adult social life. Just as children need friends their own age, so do parents.

After a divorce, many parents start dating. Children often have fantasies about their parents getting back together and they get upset if their parents start dating other people. Most parents do not get back together again, as much as their children might wish it.

They go out on dates because they like adult companionship, enjoy the attention of someone of the opposite sex, and sometimes because they hope to meet someone with whom they could have a happy marriage.

When parents start going out again, they sometimes date a number of different people. This may seem confusing to children who are used to their parents going out with only each other. Parents may date lots of different people until they meet someone who is special to them.

Occasionally, after a parent meets someone special, they may want to get married but are afraid that if they marry again, it might turn out unhappily and end in another divorce. For this reason, they may decide that they want to live together before getting married. They may want to see how their children will get along with this new person. Not everyone in our society approves of unmarried couples living together. Children sometimes are embarrassed about this situation. They may not know what to tell their friends, and their friends may tease them about it. But a lot of single parents think it is a good way to avoid making a more serious mistake, a bad second marriage.

ALMOST ALL DIVORCED PEOPLE MARRY AGAIN

Most divorced people marry again because they are sure they've finally found "the right person." Others because they think it's better for their children to live in a home with two parents.

Most people want a happy marriage. They want a second chance for themselves and for their children. The best kind of home for children to be raised in is one where there is a happy, loving marriage. A husband and wife who are kind and considerate to one another, who are able to talk to each other honestly about the things that are important to them, who are good friends as well as lovers, can share this love with the children in their home. Children who live with a happily remarried parent are far better off than when they were living with parents who didn't get along.

But putting a new family together takes a lot of time, patience, and understanding. To expect it to be perfect immediately is unrealistic. Let's take a look at two families who are trying to make it work.

Amy's mother and stepfather moved to a new state to give their marriage a fresh start. They didn't want to live near the house Amy's mother and father used to live in. They wanted to be a real family of their own. Amy and her brother provide a whole new experience for their stepfather. He was a bachelor before he married their mother, and was used to a lot of freedom and quiet. It's hard for him to get used to the fact that the children are always there, often noisy and interrupting. On the other hand, he spends a lot of time with them. He works at home and looks after them while their mother works. He worries about them, encourages them, and has a close relationship with them. He admits, though, that he and the children will never be as close as real parents and children are.

Amy and her brother have never really spent much time with a man in the house. Their own father was away a lot and they were used to having their mother to themselves. They're still having trouble sharing their mother with their stepfather.

They call their stepfather by his first name and like him a lot. But they still stand off a little. When everything is going well, they're warm and loving to him. When something's wrong, they're quick to blame it on him. They would never do that with their own father.

The children like where they live, do well in school, and seem happy except for the times when they compete for their mother's attention.

Amy's mother loves them all very much. She wants them to love one another. Sometimes she feels caught in the middle. Both the children and her husband come to her when they are angry about something the other has done. Sometimes she and her husband do not agree on what is best for the children. She'd like to be able to spend more time with her husband, and she often feels that there is never enough time for them to be alone. On the other hand, she is happy to be part of a family that does things together.

Most of the time, Amy's family finds a compromise. They try to make room for everyone's needs, and they're growing closer as time goes on. But they expected it would be easier just because they love each other.

Putting Amy's family together is easy compared to Michelle and Peter's new family.

Their father deserted their mother. One day he just left and never came back. Their mother had no money and a young set of twins. She went back to live with her parents, and they looked after Michelle and Peter while she went to work. Because she was so angry with their father, she began to use her maiden name again. Peter and Michelle used it too.

Then she met their stepfather. He had been divorced and had two children from his first marriage who lived with his first wife. Peter and Michelle were nine when their mother married again. After that, a lot of things changed very quickly.

They moved from their grandparents' house. They got not only a stepfather but two stepbrothers as well. At first, they didn't get along with the stepbrothers when they came to visit, because the house was small and everyone fought all the time. They moved again last year when their little brother was born. After he was born, they felt strange because everyone else's last name was that of their stepfather. So their stepfather adopted them in order to give them his name too.

Finally, they got along with their stepbrothers fairly well. They think sometimes that their stepfather is nicer to his own kids than he is to them. And that their mother spoils their little brother and not them. Even though they are glad that their stepfather adopted them, they would like to find out more about their own father. Especially Peter.

Their mother wants to make a new life with her husband. She tries to be loving with his children but she thinks they always compare her to their own mother.

Her husband has to work hard to support all five children, and sometimes the bills really get him down. He thinks Peter and Michelle are good kids. Sometimes when he is doing things with them, he feels lonely for his boys who live with their mother. His own boys seem to like the things he wants to do more than Peter and Michelle do. He loves their mother, though, and thinks that someday they'll all be a happy family. In the meantime, he knows they have a lot to work out.

Amy's family and Peter and Michelle's family are lucky. Even though there are a lot of complicated things to work out before things will go more smoothly, the parents love one another and are trying hard to have happy marriages.

Remarriage can be much more complicated than people realize. That's why only half of them work out.

But for the half who find happiness, remarriage is a chance that is worth taking. What could be nicer than living in a loving family? And when you think about it, why should something as special as a loving family come easily?

INDEX

ABOUT THE AUTHOR

Ann S. White is an
account executive for an
advertising agency in
Lancaster, Pennsylvania.
She is also the
mother of two children.
Once divorced, she is
now happily married
to a toy inventor.

This is her first book
for Franklin Watts.